MW01251939

Totally Lent!

A TEEN'S JOURNEY TO EASTER 2007

Chris Broslavick and Tony Pichler

Pflaum Publishing Group
Dayton, OH

Graphic design by Larissa Thompson
Cover and interior illustration by Doug Jones, www.dougjonesart.com
Edited by Karen Cannizzo

Pflaum Publishing Group
2621 Dryden Road, Suite 300
Dayton, OH 45439
800-543-4383
www.pflaum.com

ISBN 978-1-933178-44-8

Acknowledgment

The authors wish to express their appreciation to the students in Ms. Kate Deehr's religion classes at St. Bernard School in Green Bay, Wisconsin. Students previewed the manuscript for this journal and suggested insightful changes.

This book belongs to

_____ .

Introduction

Did you ever make a journey? Maybe you took a trip to your grandparents' house, to the state capitol, or to Disney World? Did any of these trips change your beliefs, your attitudes, or how you treat other people? You are about to go on a journey that just might change you. This journey is called Lent.

What do you need for this journey? This Lenten journal can be your map to guide you through the forty days of Lent—from Ash Wednesday to Easter.

Travel usually involves planes, trains, and automobiles. But in this Lenten journey, a pen will be your primary vehicle. Each day of Lent you will read a passage from the Scripture readings for the day, think about what the passage means in your life, and write your response to a related question.

This Lenten journey includes side trips. Stop at the **Do You Know...** signs to learn more about the Church. **Who's Who?** will tell you about great Christians who have traveled down this road before you. Stop at **Points of Interest** along the way to experience Lenten practices, both traditional and not so traditional.

A final thought—a runner needs discipline and encouragement to run the 26.2 miles of a marathon. You will need discipline to endure the forty days of Lent. Discipline comes from a great desire to be the very best you can be. You may also need encouragement as you journey through Lent. Don't be afraid to ask others to hold you to the discipline of reading the Bible verse and writing each day. Or, better still, find someone who can journey and journal along with you—a parent, friend, teacher, brother, or sister.

Ready?

The journey and the countdown to Easter begin now.

40 Ash Wednesday—February 21

Lent is a time for prayer, fasting, and almsgiving. *Almsgiving?*
We understand *alms* as charity, assistance, gifts for the poor, donations, contributions, or offerings. Basically, almsgiving means doing good for others. Scripture has something to say about HOW to do that.

> *"So whenever you give alms, do not sound a trumpet before you, as the hypocrites do in the synagogues and in the streets, so that they may be praised by others. Truly I tell you, they have received their reward. But when you give alms, do not let your left hand know what your right hand is doing, so that your alms may be done in secret; and your Father who sees in secret will reward you."*

Matthew 6:2-4

Give alms today "in secret." Do good for someone. Then write about your experience. Or, write out your promise to give alms. For example, begin the practice of contributing to the weekly offertory collection. Whatever, shhh!

_____

_____

_____

_____

_____

_____

_____

_____

Who's Who?

Do you ever feel that you are too young to make a difference? **Martin Luther King, Jr.,** (1929-1968) was only twenty-six years old when Rosa Parks refused to give up her seat to a white passenger on a bus in Montgomery, Alabama. King was asked to lead the organization that protested Rosa Parks' arrest with a boycott of the city's buses. King told a crowd, "As you know, my friends, there comes a time when people get tired of being trampled over by the iron feet of oppression." The crowd went wild, and the rest is history. King went on to become one of the greatest civil rights activists our country has ever known.

The Chair of Saint Peter —February 22

Jesus says, "Peter, God the Father has revealed to you who I am. I am naming you the head of my church. Your authority on earth will be honored in heaven." Do you get the idea that Peter was an important guy?

> [Jesus] said to them, "But who do you say that I am?"
> Simon Peter answered, "You are the Messiah, the
> Son of the living God." And Jesus answered him,
> "Blessed are you, Simon son of Jonah! For flesh and
> blood has not revealed this to you, but my Father in
> heaven. And I tell you, you are Peter, and on this
> rock I will build my church, and the gates of Hades
> will not prevail against it. I will give you the keys of
> the kingdom of heaven, and whatever you bind on
> earth will be bound in heaven, and whatever you
> loose on earth will be loosed in heaven."
>
> Matthew 16:15-19

Pope Benedict XVI is the successor of Peter. What is your understanding of the role of the pope in the Church?

_____

_____

_____

Do You Know...

why there are forty days in Lent? Why not fifty? Why not ten? The number *forty* had special meaning for the Jews of Jesus' time. When Moses led the Israelites out of Egypt, they camped out for forty years in the desert. This period of trial was seen as a time of preparation to enter the Promised Land. Jesus prepared to enter his public ministry by fasting for forty days and forty nights. St. Augustine wrote that Jesus remained in the tomb for forty hours as he prepared to rise from the dead. And we have the forty days of Lent to prepare for Easter.

If the prophet Isaiah were alive today, he would be a rebel. He challenged the leaders of his time for their hypocrisy. His words tell us about the true purpose for fasting.

> *Is not this the fast that I choose:*
> > *to loose the bonds of injustice,*
> > *to undo the thongs of the yoke,*
> *to let the oppressed go free,*
> > *and to break every yoke?*
> *Is it not to share your bread with the hungry,*
> > *and bring the homeless poor into your house;*
> *when you see the naked, to cover them,*
> > *and not to hide yourself from your own kin?*
> *Then your light shall break forth like the dawn....*

Isaiah 58:6-8

Maybe fasting means giving up ice cream AND putting ice cream money into the Sunday collection. Maybe fasting is giving up a movie with your friends AND spending several hours with your brother or sister. Maybe fasting is helping others AND doing it joyfully.

Isaiah is calling for us to be authentic—honest—in what we do. How can you serve others during this Lenten season?

_____

_____

_____

_____

_____

_____

_____

Who's who?

St. Katharine Drexel (1858-1955) came from one of the wealthiest families in America. When she begged Pope Leo XIII to help African and Native Americans, he replied, "Why not become a missionary yourself?" She did, founding the Sisters of the Blessed Sacrament.

The Pharisees grumbled that Jesus hung out with the wrong people.

> *The Pharisees and their scribes were complaining to his disciples, saying, "Why do you eat and drink with tax collectors and sinners?" Jesus answered, "Those who are well have no need of a physician, but those who are sick; I have come to call not the righteous but sinners to repentance."*

> Luke 5:30-32

Name the good qualities of your friends.

_____   _____

_____   _____

_____   _____

_____   _____

Do You Know...

who the Pharisees and scribes were and why the Jews hated tax collectors?
What a cast of characters is found in the Gospels! Though the Pharisees are shown in a negative light in much of the New Testament, their main intent was to help the Jews stay true to the Scriptures and to the rules and regulations that are found in the Old Testament.

Scribes were experts in Mosaic Law, the law found in the Old Testament. Similar to lawyers today, scribes were counted on to interpret the laws that Jews in Jesus' time were supposed to follow. Oftentimes in the Gospels the scribes and Pharisees are linked.

Similar to the IRS today, the tax collectors' main job was to collect taxes for the government. Unlike the IRS, tax collectors in the time of Jesus collected an additional amount, over and above the sum owed to the Roman government, to keep for themselves. Other Jews hated the greed of the tax collectors.

Point of Interest

Why Ashes on Ash Wednesday?

"Well, that 'D' is a *smudge* on his report card."

"Her behavior will *smudge* her reputation."

"The early season loss is a *smudge* on their record."

Most people think of smudges as bad things. Yet, on Ash Wednesday you get a smudge of ashes on your forehead, and this is a good thing! Why are the charred palms of Passion Sunday past smudged on your forehead?

It is from Scripture. In the Old Testament, Job put on sackcloth and ashes as a way of telling God that he was sorry for the sins he committed.

It is tradition. Christians, in the early centuries after Jesus' death and resurrection, continued the tradition of wearing sackcloth and ashes to mark the beginning of the Lenten season—the forty days of prayer, fasting, and almsgiving in preparation for Easter.

It is a sign. Ashes smudged on the forehead in the sign of the cross publicly mark the believer as a Christian. The minister says, "Turn away from sin and be faithful to the gospel" or "Remember that you are dust and to dust you shall return."

It is a practice. Ashes are an invitation to turn away from sin, to make a commitment to the Lenten practices of praying more, eating less, and giving generously.

Smudges on Ash Wednesday are good! Ashes remind us to follow Jesus faithfully during these next forty days, making our lives good and holy. This is a smudge intended to have good results!

Lent is a special opportunity. While smudges often mark where something went wrong, they also mark where to begin to make things right. Each of the activities listed on the next page can help you to clean up some smudges—to make your life better.

As you try these suggestions throughout Lent, ✔ them off.

❏ Stop into church and quietly pray for a while.

❏ Offer to lead a prayer of thanksgiving at a family meal.

❏ Receive the sacrament of Penance.

❏ Attend a parish Lenten service, such as the Stations of the Cross.

❏ Put earned money or allowance into the offertory collection.

❏ Prepare breakfast or lunch for a family member or friend.

❏ Willingly do a household chore that is not already expected of you.

❏ Write a personal note to someone who is important in your life.

❏ List 25 persons, situations, and talents for which you are grateful.

❏ Give a gift—something of yours—to another person.

❏ Apologize to someone you have offended.

❏ Tell your Mom and Dad one thing that you most appreciate about each of them.

❏ Spend some quiet time thinking about what God may be asking you to do with your life as you grow into adulthood.

❏ Choose to go without dessert or snack food for a day.

❏ Make Easter gifts for members of your family.

First Monday of Lent —February 26

What did you see when you last looked into a mirror? You should have seen an image of God! Yes, all persons are made in the image and likeness of God—your mother, your brother, your uncle, your friend, your neighbor, your dentist. You get the idea.

> *"...for I was hungry and you gave me food, I was thirsty and you gave me something to drink, I was a stranger and you welcomed me, I was naked and you gave me clothing, I was sick and you took care of me, I was in prison and you visited me.... Truly I tell you, just as you did it to one of the least of these who are members of my family, you did it to me."*

Matthew 25:35-36, 40

How will you remember that the person to whom you flashed an encouraging smile was Jesus? That the person you jabbed in the ribs was Jesus?

_____

_____

_____

_____

_____

First Tuesday of Lent —February 27

There are many ways to pray. Do you remember who taught you your first prayer? Can you still recite it?

Jesus taught his friends this familiar prayer, which we know as the Our Father.

> *Our Father in heaven,*
> *hallowed be your name.*
> *Your kingdom come.*
> *Your will be done,*
> *on earth as it is in heaven.*
>
> Matthew 6:9-10

Say the rest of the prayer aloud. In the Our Father, what is Jesus telling us about God?

_____

_____

_____

_____

_____

_____

_____

_____

_____

who's who?

Do you play in the school band or sing in the school or church choir? If the answer is yes, then **Johann Sebastian Bach** (1685-1750) is a Christian whose life might be music to your ears. A great composer, Bach created thousands of musical works. Like many other musicians of his era, Bach was a church organist whose religious faith influenced the music he composed. Two of his most famous works are *The Passion of St. Matthew* and his *Mass in B Minor*. It is interesting that just before his death he was revising a work entitled *Before Thy Throne I Come*.

As you read this passage, underline words that remind you of practices that continue in our observance of Lent today.

Jonah began to go into the city, going a day's walk. And he cried out, "Forty days more, and Nineveh shall be overthrown!" And the people of Nineveh believed God; they proclaimed a fast, and everyone, great and small, put on sackcloth.

When the news reached the king of Nineveh, he rose from his throne, removed his robe, covered himself with sackcloth, and sat in ashes. Then he had a proclamation made in Nineveh: "By the decree of the king and his nobles: No human being or animal, no herd or flock, shall taste anything. They shall not feed, nor shall they drink water. Human beings and animals shall be covered with sackcloth, and they shall cry mightily to God. All shall turn from their evil ways and from the violence that is in their hands. Who knows? God may relent and change his mind; he may turn from his fierce anger, so that we do not perish."

When God saw what they did, how they turned from their evil ways, God changed his mind about the calamity that he had said he would bring upon them; and he did not do it.

Jonah 3:4-10

The people of the Old Testament used sackcloth and ashes to show their repentance. How do you show that you are sorry for wrongdoing?

_____

_____

_____

_____

It's a "Now!" world. Hungry? Stop at a fast-food restaurant; you'll have a meal in minutes. Math problem? Pull out your calculator. Bored? TV, MP3 players, and PlayStations provide instant entertainment.

Here we learn Jesus' strategy for finding solutions.

> *"Ask, and it will be given you; search, and you will find;*
> *knock, and the door will be opened for you. For everyone*
> *who asks receives, and everyone who searches finds,*
> *and for everyone who knocks, the door will be opened."*
>
> Matthew 7:7-8

What is Jesus telling you about solving problems?

_____

_____

_____

_____

_____

_____

_____

Do You Know...

why Sundays are not counted in the forty days of Lent?
Each Sunday is a celebration of the paschal or Easter mystery—Christ's passion, death, resurrection, and ascension into glory. This is the foundation of our faith. So on Sundays in Lent, we take a break from penitential practices to celebrate Sunday as a holy day to commemorate our deliverance from sin and death.

Did you ever have a change of heart or change your mind?

The prophet Ezekiel delivers a message that you already know. If you are good, you will enjoy eternal life. If you choose evil, well.... Whatever you choose, you can always change your direction.

> *But if the wicked turn away from all their sins that they have committed and keep all my statutes and do what is lawful and right, they shall surely live; they shall not die. None of the transgressions that they have committed shall be remembered against them; for the righteousness that they have done they shall live.*
> Ezekiel 18:21-22

Knowing that God forgets wrongdoing when it turns to good, what would you like to change for the good?

_____

_____

_____

_____

_____

If you are mean to me, I am going to be mean to you. If you do a favor for me, I will do the same for you. That makes us even! Well, it WAS even until Jesus came along and tipped the scales!

> *"You have heard that it was said, 'You shall love your neighbor and hate your enemy.' But I say to you, Love your enemies and pray for those who persecute you, so that you may be children of your Father in heaven....For if you love those who love you, what reward do you have?"*
>
> Matthew 5:43-45, 46

What do you think about what Jesus is saying? How difficult is it to live out this teaching? Is it actually possible?

_____

_____

_____

_____

_____

Do You Know...

if you are a Gentile?
Unless you are a person from the Jewish religion, the answer is "Yes!" For the Jews, anyone who is not a Jew is a Gentile. So, a person who calls himself/herself a Christian is considered a Gentile.

Point of Interest

Make a Pilgrimage Without Leaving Home!

If you ever journeyed to an important religious place, such as a cathedral or shrine, you would call that trip a pilgrimage, a journey of faith.

After the death and resurrection of Jesus, early Christians made pilgrimages to Jerusalem to walk the Way of the Cross. They traced the journey of Jesus as he carried his cross through the streets of Jerusalem on his way to Golgotha, where he was crucified. These pilgrims believed that by walking in the footsteps of Jesus, they were becoming more like Jesus.

When the Holy Land, including Jerusalem, came under Muslim control, Christians could no longer make pilgrimages to Jerusalem to walk the Way of the Cross.

Beginning in the eleventh century, Christian armies tried to regain the Holy Land. This struggle, called the Crusades, lasted for many years. The Christian soldiers in Jerusalem walked the Way of the Cross, just as the early Christians had. When they returned home, they made miniature statues that represented the steps Jesus took on the way to his death. The soldiers brought the Way of the Cross back home. This observance became known as the Stations of the Cross, with Christians stopping at each "station" to remember an important part of Jesus' journey.

In 1742, Pope Benedict XIV set the number of stations at fourteen. Today some churches have added a fifteenth station for the resurrection of Jesus. The fifteen Stations of the Cross are listed on the next page. Use the code to fill in the stations that are missing.

A	B	C	D	E	F	G	H	I	J	K	L	M
✠	♌	ᴄ᷌	♎	♏	♐	♑	♒	🖐	☺	&	●	◗

N	O	P	Q	R	S	T	U	V	W	X	Y	Z
■	✪	✈	⌀	□	🔔	↑	◆	❖	⊓	⊠	◗	⌘

Decode the Stations of the Cross!

1st Station: Jesus is condemned to death.

2nd Station: ↑≋ℳ ⌇⃝▢✪△△ ᳵ△ ●✠ᳵ♎ ◆↝✪▪ ☺ℳ△◆△

____ _____ __ ____ _____ _____.

3rd Station: Jesus falls the first time.

4th Station: ☺ℳ△◆△ ◯ℳℳ↑△ ≋ᳵ△ ◯✪↑≋ℳ▢ ◯✠▢◗

_____ _____ ___ _____, _____.

5th Station: Simon of Cyrene helps Jesus carry the cross.

6th Station: Veronica wipes Jesus' face.

7th Station: ☺ℳ△◆△ ᳵ✠●●△ ᳵ✪▢ ↑≋ℳ △ℳ⌇⃝▪♎ ↑ᳵ◯ℳ

_____ _____ ___ ___ _____ ____.

8th Station: Jesus meets the women of Jerusalem.

9th Station: Jesus falls the third time.

10th Station: Jesus is stripped of his garments.

11th Station: ☺ℳ△◆△ ᳵ△ ▪✠ᳵ●ℳ♎ ↑✪ ↑≋ℳ ⌇⃝▢✪△△

_____ __ _____ __ ___ _____.

12th Station: Jesus dies on the cross.

13th Station: Jesus' body is taken down from the cross.

14th Station: ☺ℳ△◆△ ᳵ△ ●✠ᳵ♎ ᳵ▪ ↑≋ℳ ↑✪◯𝒮

_____ __ _____ __ ___ _____.

15th Station: ☺ℳ△◆△ ▢ᳵ△ℳ△ ᳵ▢✪◯ ↑≋ℳ ♎ℳ✠♎

_____ _____ ___ ___ _____.

19

30 Second Monday of Lent— March 5

Have you heard the saying, "What goes around, comes around"? It suggests that your attitudes and actions have a rebound effect. If you are good to others, they are likely to be good to you. When you cause injury to someone, you may find yourself a victim of someone's hurtful words or actions.

Jesus tells us something very similar.

> "Do not judge, and you will not be judged; do not condemn, and you will not be condemned. Forgive, and you will be forgiven; give, and it will be given to you. A good measure, pressed down, shaken together, running over, will be put into your lap; for the measure you give will be the measure you get back."
>
> Luke 6:37-38

Find a clear jar or bowl. At the end of the day, put a penny in the jar for every kind word or act directed toward you throughout the day. Do this through the remainder of the Lenten season.

What does the number of pennies imply about YOU? What will you do with the pennies you collect?

_____

_____

_____

_____

_____

_____

Wash yourselves; make yourselves clean;
remove the evil of your doings
from before my eyes;
cease to do evil,
learn to do good;
seek justice,
rescue the oppressed,
defend the orphan,
plead for the widow.

Isaiah 1:16-17

Clean your room. Eat breakfast. Dress for the weather. Do your home-work. Study for the math test. Keep your grades up. Get off the internet. Do not accept rides from strangers. Tell someone where you are going.

Is the prophet Isaiah living at your house? It might seem that way!

What do you think? What was the purpose of Isaiah's message? What is the purpose of the instructions you get at home?

_____

_____

_____

_____

_____

_____

_____

_____

who's who?

Can you recite the Nicene Creed, the Creed that we say at Mass each Sunday? **St. Gregory of Nyssa** (330-395) is one of the theologians credited with defending the Nicene Creed against the Arians, who didn't believe that Jesus was truly divine. In his writings, St. Gregory supported the doctrine of the Trinity, which tells us that there are three divine persons in one God—Father, Son, and Holy Spirit.

Second Wednesday of Lent— March 7

Then the mother of the sons of Zebedee…asked a favor of [Jesus]. And he said to her, "What do you want?" She said to him, "Declare that these two sons of mine will sit, one at your right hand and one at your left, in your kingdom." But Jesus answered, "You do not know what you are asking. Are you able to drink the cup that I am about to drink?" They said to him, "We are able." He said to them, "You will indeed drink my cup, but to sit at my right hand and at my left, this is not mine to grant, but it is for those for whom it has been prepared by my Father."

… "You know that the rulers of the Gentiles lord it over them, and their great ones are tyrants over them. It will not be so among you; but whoever wishes to be great among you must be your servant, and whoever wishes to be first among you must be your slave; just as the Son of Man came not to be served but to serve; and to give his life as a ransom for many."

Matthew 20:20-23, 25-28

What have you done over the past few days that would suggest you are following Jesus' advice about how to be great?

_____

_____

_____

Do You Know…

that slavery is talked about in Scripture?
While slavery was one of the issues that caused the Civil War, the possession of persons as property didn't originate in the United States. Unfortunately, slavery was also part of the society in which Jesus lived. The issue of slavery comes up in several places in Scripture, with the message that slaves and owners are to be seen as equals.

Second Thursday of Lent— March 8

"I didn't do anything!" Have those words ever come out of your mouth? Well, there is no room in the kingdom for the passive Christian!

> *"There was a rich man who was dressed in purple and fine linen and who feasted sumptuously every day. And at his gate lay a poor man named Lazarus, covered with sores, who longed to satisfy his hunger with what fell from the rich man's table; even the dogs would come and lick his sores. The poor man died and was carried away by the angels to be with Abraham. The rich man also died and was buried. In Hades, where he was being tormented, he looked up and saw Abraham far away with Lazarus by his side. He called out, 'Father Abraham, have mercy on me, and send Lazarus to dip the tip of his finger in water and cool my tongue; for I am in agony in these flames.' But Abraham said, 'Child, remember that during your lifetime you received your good things, and Lazarus in like manner evil things; but now he is comforted here, and you are in agony.' "*

Luke 16:19-25

Read your parish bulletin and talk to your parents and members of the parish staff to find out what you can do to share your "good things" with those less fortunate than you. Write here what you will do. Be sure to follow through.

_____

_____

_____

_____

_____

"…There was a landowner who planted a vineyard, put a fence around it, dug a wine press in it, and built a watch-tower. Then he leased it to tenants and went to another country. When the harvest time had come, he sent his slaves to the tenants to collect his produce. But the tenants seized his slaves and beat one, killed another, and stoned another. Again he sent other slaves, more than the first; and they treated them in the same way. Finally he sent his son to them, saying, 'They will respect my son.' But when the tenants saw the son, they said to themselves, 'This is the heir; come, let us kill him and get his inheritance.' So they seized him, threw him out of the vineyard, and killed him. Now when the owner of the vineyard comes, what will he do to those tenants?" [The chief priests and elders] said to him, *"He will put those wretches to a miserable death, and lease the vineyard to other tenants who will give him the produce at the harvest time."*

Matthew 21:33-41

In what ways are the landowner and God alike?

_____

_____

_____

_____

Do You Know...

why so many vineyards are mentioned in the Bible?
Vineyards are some of the most frequently mentioned pieces of real estate in the Scriptures and for good reason. We might choose to drink milk, water, lemonade, or iced tea with our meals. But because grapes were a primary crop of the Jews in Jesus' time, wine—fermented, crushed grapes—was their drink of choice.

25 Second Saturday of Lent— March 10

Dread. Sheer dread. Have you ever felt it? It happens when you break your mom's crystal plate, cause someone to be injured, or are haunted by having said something awful. And you have to face what you've done. You have to make your apology. How do you want to be received by the person you have offended?

Micah tells us how God responds to sinners.

> Who is a God like you, pardoning iniquity
>> and passing over the transgression
>> of the remnant of your possession?
> He does not retain his anger forever,
>> because he delights in showing clemency.
> He will again have compassion upon us;
>> he will tread our iniquities under foot.
> You will cast all our sins
>> into the depths of the sea.
>
> Micah 7:18-19

Describe the most compassionate, caring person you know.

_____

_____

_____

_____

_____

_____

_____

_____

Who's Who?

Blessed Mother Teresa of Calcutta (1910-1997) is recognized around the world for her personal holiness and for her compassion for the poor. But in today's divided world, she is also an important symbol of the unity of all God's people. As a Roman Catholic Albanian who joined the Irish Sisters of Loretto, she knew what it was like to be in the minority. But her great charity won her first the acceptance and then the love of millions of non-Christians in India.

Point of Interest

Travel Through the Church Year!

You've probably learned about the five senses—smell, touch, taste, hearing, and sight—in science class. Did you ever think about how you use the five senses at Mass? Match each of the senses with the activity or object that is part of the Mass. You can check your answers at the bottom of the next page.

a. Sight ___Incense
b. Hearing ___The color of vestments
c. Smell ___The host and wine
d. Touch ___Songs and hymns
e. Taste ___Sign of Peace

To get an idea of how our senses help us to be fully aware of God's presence, let's focus on sight, especially on the colors that we see at Mass during various times of the year.

Your school operates from August or September to May or June; this is an academic year. Businesses operate on a fiscal year. One month is designated as the beginning of the fiscal year and all records of financial gains or losses are kept based on that date. The calendar of the Church is the liturgical year. Beginning with the first Sunday of Advent—usually in late November—the Church year, or liturgical year, has many different seasons and holy days.

Advent—four weeks (ends at Christmas)

Christmas—twelve days (ends at Epiphany)

Ordinary Time (This season has thirty-three or thirty-four Sundays, depending on the date of Easter, and is celebrated in two parts. The first part begins after Epiphany and ends with Ash Wednesday.)

Lent—forty days plus six Sundays (ends with Easter)

Easter—fifty days (ends with Pentecost)

Ordinary Time (This second stretch of Ordinary Time fills the time between Pentecost and the first Sunday of Advent.)

Each season of the liturgical year is marked by a special color to signify that we have moved into a special time. The colors of the vestments worn by the priest help us to use our sense of sight to experience something special.

Advent—violet (purple)

Christmas—white

Ordinary Time—green

Lent—violet (purple)

Easter—white

Good Friday and Pentecost and other special days—red

The colors are meant to signify to all Catholic Christians that the Church is celebrating a particular season or time of the liturgical year. So, the next time you go to Mass, figure out what season the Church is celebrating by noticing the priest's vestments or the altar cloth. Color helps us encounter God in a different way.

Color Me Purple!

After all, it is Lent. And, perhaps a visual reminder will help sustain your awareness of this season. How can you do that?

✓ Check your clothing. Do you have anything purple? Consider wearing purple occasionally during the Lenten season.

✓ How about a Lenten dessert for your family? Make purple Jell-O by mixing a box of blue Jell-O with a box of red Jell-O and following the package directions. The result should be a purple gelatin.

✓ Are you artistic? Consider doing an art piece in any media featuring the color purple and the symbols of Lent. Display your work in your room or your home as a reminder of the season of Lent.

✓ Do you enjoy plants or flowers? Or, do you enjoy giving plants or flowers? Perhaps you could find a purple plant or flower for your home or to give as a gift. Think about it!

We have all five senses working at Mass.
If you answered c, a, e, b, d, you are absolutely correct. Give yourself an "A"!

27

Naaman, the commander of an army, had leprosy. He made his way to the house of the prophet Elisha who sent a messenger to Naaman telling him how to be cured. It was a simple task: Wash in the river Jordan. But Naaman became enraged and went away.

> *But his servants approached and said to him. "Father, if the prophet had commanded you to do something difficult, would you not have done it? How much more, when all he said to you was, 'Wash, and be clean'?" So he went down and immersed himself seven times in the Jordan, according to the word of the man of God; his flesh was restored like the flesh of a young boy, and he was clean.*

2 Kings 5:13-14

Typical, isn't it? Would you not be more willing to run out into the street to save the life of a young child than you are to carry your dirty clothes to the washer? The point: Following God often involves doing simple everyday things.

Who's Who?

Have you or your parents ever dropped off used items at a St. Vincent de Paul container or store? We can thank **St. Louise de Marillac** (1591-1660) for her role in establishing this helping organization. In seventeenth-century Paris, St. Louise de Marillac and St. Vincent de Paul joined together to help the poor by forming the Daughters of Charity. Later, the St. Vincent de Paul Society would be formed for the same purpose. St. Louise de Marillac urged Christians to love and honor the poor as they would Christ himself.

Why is it sometimes difficult to do simple everyday things?

_____

_____

_____

_____

_____

_____

_____

_____

Forgiveness, as an expression of love, has no limits. It is not like the money in your pocket or the soda in a can. You can always reach down into your heart and find forgiveness. You can pour it out to others any time you choose. Jesus makes this point to Peter.

> Then Peter came and said to [Jesus], "Lord, if another member of the church sins against me, how often should I forgive? As many as seven times?" Jesus said to him, "Not seven times, but I tell you, seventy-seven times."
>
> Matthew 18:21-22

Why do you think Peter asked Jesus about forgiveness? Peter wants to know how many times he must forgive another member of the church. Who do you need to forgive?

_____

_____

_____

_____

_____

Do You Know...

what numbers had special significance for people in Jesus' time?
In today's world we use numbers for everything. The stock market in New York uses numbers. Statistics in sports are endless. People have identification numbers. In Jesus' time, certain numbers carried special meanings. The number 666 stood for the beast in the Book of Revelation. The number 3 meant completeness, as seen in the complete denial of Jesus by Peter (three times) or the times that Jesus asks Peter if he loves Jesus (three times). The number 7 stood for perfection. So, in today's reading, when Jesus tells his followers to forgive one another seventy-seven times, he is calling for them to move almost beyond perfection.

In this passage, Jesus is making a point about the importance of the law—the commandments. But he is making a greater point about giving good or bad example—what he calls "teaching others."

> *"Do not think that I have come to abolish the law*
> *or the prophets; I have come not to abolish but to fulfill.*
> *For truly I tell you, until heaven and earth pass away,*
> *not one letter, not one stroke of a letter, will pass from*
> *the law until all is accomplished. Therefore, whoever*
> *breaks one of the least of these commandments, and*
> *teaches others to do the same, will be called least in the*
> *kingdom of heaven; but whoever does them and teaches*
> *them will be called great in the kingdom of heaven."*
> Matthew 5:17-19

What are you teaching others? Write about a time in which you think you were a good example.

_____

_____

_____

_____

Do You Know...

what the Jews called the Ten Commandments?
The Ten Commandments were given to Moses at Mount Sinai (Exodus 20:2-17 and Deuteronomy 5:1-22). Originally, the Jews called the Ten Commandments the Decalogue, or Ten Words. *Deca* is Greek for ten, and *logue* means words. Because little was written down, and people relied on storytelling to teach one another, the best way to memorize the Ten Commandments was to remember one important word from each commandment.

Jeremiah is someone you need to know about. He was a kid like you when God called him to be a prophet. He tried to get out of doing the job, but God wouldn't let him. What was worse, he had to deliver a message the people didn't want to hear. Here's part of what God told Jeremiah.

> But this command I gave them, "Obey my voice, and I will be your God, and you shall be my people; and walk only in the way that I command you, so that it may be well with you." Yet they did not obey or incline their ear, but, in the stubbornness of their evil will, they walked in their own counsels, and looked backward rather than forward. From the day that your ancestors came out of the land of Egypt until this day, I have persistently sent all my servants the prophets to them, day after day; yet they did not listen to me, or pay attention, but they stiffened their necks. They did worse than their ancestors did.
>
> So you shall speak all these words to them, but they will not listen to you. You shall call to them, but they will not answer you. You shall say to them: This is the nation that did not obey the voice of the LORD their God, and did not accept discipline; truth has perished; it is cut off from their lips.
>
> Jeremiah 7:23-28

How does it feel to have people older than you paying attention to what you say?

_____

_____

_____

_____

_____

_____

Third Friday of Lent— March 16

The people of Israel strayed from God. They worshiped idols and oppressed the poor. Through the prophet Hosea, God reprimands his people.

> *It is I who answer and look after you.*
> *I am like an evergreen cypress;*
>   *your faithfulness comes from me.*
> *Those who are wise understand these things;*
>   *those who are discerning know them.*
> *For the ways of the LORD are right,*
>   *and the upright walk in them,*
>   *but transgressors stumble in them.*
>
>   Hosea 14:8-9

Who's who?

Prophets are called by God to speak in his name. The task of Old Testament prophets like Hosea was to call people back to God's covenant, the way to salvation. **John the Baptist** (first century) was a prophet of the New Testament, but "more than a prophet" (Luke 7:26). John the Baptist fulfilled the role of a prophet—to challenge people to repent and change their ways. But he was also the messenger sent by God to prepare the way for Jesus, who would fulfill God's promise of salvation.

To whose voice are you listening? How is a caring person encouraging you to be your best?

_____

_____

_____

_____

_____

_____

_____

_____

_____

_____

Third Saturday of Lent— March 17 (Feast of St. Patrick)

Oh, it's a temptation, isn't it, to find little ways to see ourselves as just a bit better than another person?

The scene is the temple. Two men, one a Pharisee and the other a tax collector, are praying.

"The Pharisee, standing by himself, was praying thus, 'God, I thank you that I am not like other people: thieves, rogues, adulterers, or even like this tax collector. I fast twice a week; I give a tenth of all my income.' But the tax collector, standing far off, would not even look up to heaven, but was beating his breast and saying, 'God, be merciful to me, a sinner!' I tell you, this [tax collector] went down to his home justified rather than the [Pharisee]; for all who exalt themselves will be humbled, but all who humble themselves will be exalted."

Luke 18:11-14

What do you think it means to be humble?

_____

_____

_____

_____

_____

_____

_____

_____

Who's Who?

Shamrocks. Leprechauns. Green clothes. Driving snakes out of Ireland. These are just some of the things that come to mind today as we celebrate the feast of St. Patrick.

St. Patrick (387-461) was a missionary who converted Ireland to Christianity. He used the shamrock to teach the people about the Trinity—three persons in one God. For more than thirty years, Patrick wandered the Irish countryside as a bishop, establishing churches, dioceses, and monasteries.

Point of Interest

Play the Catholic Millionaire Game!

For Christians, Lent and Easter are the most important season and holi-day of the year. Why? Think about it. If Jesus had not died on the cross and risen from the dead, would his birth be as important as it is today?

Many symbols and traditions make this time of year meaningful for Christians. How much do you know about Lenten and Easter symbols and traditions? Circle the correct answers for these questions—and win!

1. The custom of twisting dough into a pretzel shape was started by:
a. a baker
b. a mother of 5 children
c. a monk
d. a football player
(Your correct answer is worth $1,000!)

2. The pretzel's shape symbolizes:
a. arms folded in prayer
b. a person hugging himself/herself
c. a "Y" in a circle
d. none of the above
($2,000)

3. The custom of baking pretzels began in:
a. the United States
b. Mexico
c. Australia
d. Germany
($4,000)

4. How many pounds of pretzels do people in the United States consume each year?
a. 1,000 pounds
b. 1 million pounds
c. 10 million pounds
d. 400 million pounds
($8,000)

5. What ingredient is not found in pretzels?
a. water
b. flour
c. nutmeg
d. salt
($16,000)

6. Originally, Easter eggs were painted bright colors to:
a. symbolize the bright sunlight of spring
b. make eggs easier to find on Easter egg hunts
c. match the bright colors of Easter clothing
d. none of the above
($32,000)

7. In Greece, people traditionally colored Easter eggs red because:
a. red is the national color of Greece
b. red symbolizes the blood of Jesus
c. red is a nice color
d. the first person to color eggs in Greece only had red dye
($64,000)

8. *Pysanki* eggs are:
a. eggs from the *Pysanki*, a wild animal in the Amazon
b. eggs that are hard-boiled and placed on salads
c. eggs that are decorated with intricate designs
d. eggs purchased from the *Pysanki* grocery store
($128,000)

9. The bunny is an Easter symbol because:
a. this fast animal symbolizes the speed with which people try to find Easter eggs
b. this fertile animal symbolizes life
c. it makes for a great design in chocolate
d. none of the above
($500,000)

10. The egg is an Easter symbol because:
a. it would be hard to dye peanuts
b. eggs and bunnies just seem to go together
c. eggs symbolize new life
d. whoever heard of chocolate Easter footballs
($1,000,000)

You can check your answers on page 63. But please don't look until you've tried to answer all the questions on your own.

◆ How many of the ten questions did you answer correctly?
◆ How much did you win?
◆ What did you learn?

18 Solemnity of St. Joseph
—March 19

Have you ever had a problem or a situation that you did not know how to handle? If you were lucky, someone came along and said something that gave you a whole new understanding of the circumstances. St. Joseph found himself in just such a situation.

> ...When [Jesus'] mother Mary had been engaged to Joseph, but before they lived together, she was found to be with child from the Holy Spirit. Her husband Joseph, being a righteous man and unwilling to expose her to public disgrace, planned to dismiss her quietly. But just when he had resolved to do this, an angel of the Lord appeared to him in a dream and said, "Joseph, son of David, do not be afraid to take Mary as your wife, for the child conceived in her is from the Holy Spirit."
>
> Matthew 1:18-20

Who's who?

For a guy who played such an important role in the life of Jesus, **St. Joseph** (first century) sure didn't receive much press! Joseph is mentioned in only two of the four Gospels—Matthew and Luke. It wasn't until the sixteenth century that Christians started to pay attention to him as a model of faith. Finally, in 1870, Pope Pius IX declared him Patron of the Universal Church.

Don't forget to celebrate Joseph's other feast day—the feast of St. Joseph the Worker on May 1.

Describe a difficult situation that you have been in. Who was your angel—the person who guided you to a good solution?

_____

_____

_____

_____

_____

_____

_____

_____

Faith. Desire. Persistence. Imagine believing that something can happen, wanting it enough to be ready to go after it, and then, trying over and over and over again.

> *When Jesus saw him lying there and knew that he had been there a long time, he said to him, "Do you want to be made well?" The sick man answered him, "Sir, I have no one to put me into the pool when the water is stirred up; and while I am making my way, someone else steps down ahead of me." Jesus said to him, "Stand up, take your mat and walk." At once the man was made well, and he took up his mat and began to walk.*
>
> John 5:6-9

What goal do you have? What do you think you'll need to do to show the faith, desire, and persistence to reach this goal?

_____

_____

_____

_____

_____

_____

_____

_____

_____

_____

_____

Who's Who?

Talk about conversions—changes of the heart and mind! When **Archbishop Oscar Romero** (1917-1980) was named Archbishop of San Salvador in El Salvador, he was known as pious and conservative. Nothing in his background suggested that he might challenge the forces in his country that were oppressing poor people. Yet, after the assassination of his friend, Rutilio Grande, a Jesuit priest, Romero changed dramatically. He became a voice for the voiceless and a champion for the poor. In 1980, Romero was killed for his beliefs while presiding at Mass. Before his death, Romero wrote: "A bishop will die, but the Church of God—the people—will never die."

Thus says the LORD:
In a time of favor I have answered you,
    on a day of salvation I have helped you;
I have kept you and given you
    as a covenant to the people,
to establish the land,
    to apportion the desolate heritages;
saying to the prisoners, "Come out,"
    to those who are in darkness, "Show yourselves."
They shall feed along the ways,
    on all the bare heights shall be their pasture;
they shall not hunger or thirst,
    neither scorching wind nor
        sun shall strike them down,
for he who has pity on them will lead them,
    and by springs of water will guide them.
And I will turn all my mountains into a road,
    and my highways shall be raised up.
                                    Isaiah 49:8-11

In this passage, Isaiah is telling us that God takes care of people. God is ever vigilant, ever present, ever caring.

Write about a time when you or someone close to you experienced God's caring presence.

_____

_____

_____

_____

_____

_____

15 Fourth Thursday of Lent— March 22

When was the last time you pleaded with your parents for a privilege or a possession that you could not live without? You clarified your reasons, you made a successful case, and you received what you wanted.

When requests—big or small, urgent or not-so-urgent—are directed toward God, it is called prayer. This is how Moses prayed to God.

> *"Turn from your fierce wrath; change your mind and do not bring disaster on your people. Remember Abraham, Isaac, and Israel, your servants, how you swore to them by your own self, saying to them, 'I will multiply your descendants like the stars of heaven, and all this land that I have promised I will give to your descendants, and they shall inherit it forever.' " And the LORD changed his mind about the disaster that he planned to bring on his people.*
>
> Exodus 32:12-14

How do you pray? Or, why do you pray?

_____

_____

_____

_____

_____

_____

_____

_____

_____

Who's Who?

Who is the bravest person you have ever met? **Harriet Tubman** (1820?-1913) is among the bravest Christians in U.S. history. A slave living in Maryland before the Civil War, Harriet escaped to freedom via the Underground Railroad, a network of good people who helped slaves on their journey to becoming free. One of the most famous "conductors" on the Underground Railroad, Harriet used her freedom to help hundreds, including her own parents, to escape slavery.

14 Fourth Friday of Lent—
March 23

He is! He isn't! He is. He isn't. He is. He isn't. The great debate was whether or not Jesus was the Messiah.

> Now some of the people of Jerusalem were saying,
> "Is not this the man whom they are trying to kill?
> And here he is, speaking openly, but they say
> nothing to him! Can it be that the authorities really
> know that this is the Messiah? Yet we know where
> this man is from; but when the Messiah comes,
> no one will know where he is from." Then Jesus
> cried out as he was teaching in the temple,
> "You know me, and you know where I am from.
> I have not come on my own. But the one who sent
> me is true, and you do not know him. I know him,
> because I am from him, and he sent me."
>
> John 7:25-29

How would you explain Jesus' response?

_____

_____

_____

_____

Do You Know...

what *Messiah* means?
Messiah is a Hebrew word that means "Anointed One." The same word in Greek is *Christos*, or Christ. In the Old Testament, kings and high priests were anointed with oil as they began their leadership in the name of God. Certain Old Testament writers looked forward to a Messiah, one who would lead the Jews from the rule of Rome. Jesus was seen as this person—the Messiah, the Anointed One. *Christ* is not Jesus' last name. Rather, it is a title that speaks of Jesus' important place in the reign of God.

Nicodemus was a Pharisee and a leader of the people. He had also secretly come to know Jesus. In this passage from John, the Jewish leaders are trying to make the point that Jesus could not possibly be the Christ or a prophet. Nicodemus, as any good lawyer, appeals to the law to save Jesus. But no one will listen.

> *Nicodemus, who had gone to Jesus before, and who was one of them [a Pharisee and leader], asked, "Our law does not judge people without first giving them a hearing to find out what they are doing, does it?" They replied, "Surely you are not also from Galilee, are you? Search and you will see that no prophet is to arise from Galilee."*
>
> John 7:50-52

How does it feel when no one will listen to what you believe to be true?

_____

_____

_____

_____

_____

_____

_____

_____

Point of Interest

Experience a 13th Century Catholic Devotion!

Can you imagine eating a plate of spaghetti without a knife and fork? How about writing a paper for English class without paper, a pen, or a computer? We use many objects or tools every day to make life easier.

We also use many aids to help us pray—the Bible, images of Jesus, and even this Lenten journal. Another aid that you probably have seen, and maybe even used, is the rosary.

The rosary is a string of beads that are grouped into five sets of ten beads separated by a single bead. A cross and a small set of beads (1-3-1) connect the ends of the string forming a loop.

The five sets of beads represent different "mysteries," or events, in the life of Jesus. As you pray with each set of beads, you reflect on one of these events. A total of twenty events are divided into four groups. The Joyful Mysteries recount the events from the angel announcing that Mary would be the mother of our savior to the finding of Jesus in the Temple. The Mysteries of Light, or Luminous Mysteries, recall special times in Jesus' adult life—his Baptism to the first Eucharist. The Sorrowful Mysteries recall the suffering and death of Jesus. The Glorious Mysteries recall events from the resurrection to the crowning of Mary in heaven.

So, how do you pray the rosary?

1. Make the Sign of the Cross.
2. While holding the cross of the rosary, recite the Apostles' Creed.
3. On the first bead, pray the Our Father.
4. Pray the Hail Mary on each of the next three beads.
5. Pray the Glory Be.
6. Name the mystery—for example, the agony in the garden.
7. Pray an Our Father on the next bead.
8. Pray the Hail Marys on the next ten beads.
9. Complete the decade (ten beads) by praying the Glory Be.
10. Repeat steps 6 through 9 for each mystery in the group.

Pray the Rosary Today!

If you do not have or cannot borrow a rosary, you can make one. Take a length of cord or yarn and tie knots in the pattern of the beads illustrated here. Use your creativity to fashion a cross.

Pray the Sorrowful Mysteries. These are the last scriptural events of the Lenten season. As you pray the ten Hail Marys for each sorrowful mystery, think about what you know and have learned about that particular event.

The Sorrowful Mysteries

The agony of Christ in the garden (Mark 14:32-36)
The scourging of Jesus (John 18:28-38; 19:1)
The crowning with thorns (Mark 15:16-20)
The carrying of the cross (John 19:14-17)
The crucifixion and death of Jesus (Luke 23:33-34; 39-46)

Not feeling too confident?

Invite someone to join you or join a friend or family member for whom the rosary is an important devotion. Or, check your parish bulletin for times when parishioners gather to pray the rosary.

Annunciation of the Lord— March 26

The feast of the Annunciation celebrates the great faith of a young person. A young woman from a small town learns about God's plan for her and then courageously accepts the plan.

You know this story. An angel visits Mary, who is engaged to Joseph. The angel tells Mary that she is going to have a baby, "the Son of the Most High." Mary is very perplexed and asks how this can happen since she is not yet even married. The angel explains that the power of the Holy Spirit will make this possible, just as the Spirit has already made it possible for Mary's cousin, Elizabeth, to have a child in her old age.

As unbelievable as all of this may have seemed, Mary's faith in God was unwavering. The angel tells Mary, "For nothing will be impossible with God." Mary replies, "Here am I, the servant of the Lord; let it be with me according to your word." (Luke 1:37-38)

How do you think you will learn about God's plan for you? How do you think you will respond?

_____

_____

_____

_____

Do You Know...
what small town Mary was from?

We don't know much about Nazareth, the town where Mary and Joseph lived and where Jesus grew up. But the Gospel of Luke tells us what happened when Jesus returned to his hometown as a grown-up. When the people heard they would not get any special treatment from Jesus, they became very angry. They drove him out of town and tried to throw him over a cliff. To find out what happened next, read Luke 4:30.

Fifth Tuesday of Lent— March 27

In many ways the Old Testament prefigured—suggested beforehand—the events of the New Testament. Look for an image in this passage that parallels the event of Jesus' crucifixion.

> *From Mount [Horeb] they set out by the way to the Red Sea, to go around the land of Edom; but the people became impatient on the way. The people spoke against God and against Moses, "Why have you brought us up out of Egypt to die in the wilderness? For there is no food and no water, and we detest this miserable food." Then the LORD sent poisonous serpents among the people, and they bit the people, so that many Israelites died. The people came to Moses and said, "We have sinned by speaking against the LORD and against you; pray to the LORD to take away the serpents from us." So Moses prayed for the people. And the LORD said to Moses, "Make a poisonous serpent, and set it on a pole; and everyone who is bitten shall look at it and live." So Moses made a serpent of bronze, and put it upon a pole; and whenever a serpent bit someone, that person would look at the serpent of bronze and live.*
>
> Numbers 21:4-9

Compare the pole with the serpent of the Old Testament with the cross of the New Testament.

_____

_____

_____

_____

_____

_____

King Nebuchadnezzar told Sadrach, Meshach, and Abednego to worship a golden statue. If they didn't, he threatened that they would be bound and thrown into a fire. They refused because they believed God would deliver them.

> *Hearing them sing, and amazed at seeing them alive, King Nebuchadnezzar rose up quickly. He said to his counselors, "Was it not three men that we threw bound into the fire?" They answered the king, "True, O king." He replied, "But I see four men unbound, walking in the middle of the fire, and they are not hurt; and the fourth has the appearance of a god." …Nebuchadnezzar said, "Blessed be the God of Shadrach, Meshach, and Abednego, who has sent his angel and delivered his servants who trusted in him. They disobeyed the king's command and yielded up their bodies rather than serve and worship any god except their own God."*

Daniel 3:91-92, 95

Read the complete story in chapter 3 of the Book of Daniel, and imagine the special effects that might be used in a film version.

Who's Who?

Talk about courage! In 1953, **Thea Bowman** (1937-1990) entered an all-white convent and brought her African-American heritage and unique spirit to all she met. "What does it mean to be black and Catholic?" she asked. "It means… I bring myself, my black self, all that I am, all that I have, all that I hope to become. I bring my whole history, my traditions, my experience, my culture, my African-American song and dance and gesture and movement and teaching and preaching and healing and responsibility as gift to the Church."

Write about a time when you stood up for a belief or value of your own.

_____

_____

_____

_____

_____

_____

_____

_____

Our names are important to us, but names had a special significance in the Old Testament. When God changed Abram's name, it signaled important changes in his life.

> ...and God said to [Abram], "As for me, this is my covenant with you: You shall be the ancestor of a multitude of nations. No longer shall your name be Abram, but your name shall be Abraham; for I have made you the ancestor of a multitude of nations. I will make you exceedingly fruitful; and I will make nations of you, and kings shall come from you. I will establish my covenant between me and you, and your offspring after you throughout their generations, for an everlasting covenant, to be God to you and to your offspring after you."
>
> Genesis 17:3-7

How did your parents choose your name?

What does your name mean?

How do you show those characteristics?

_____

_____

_____

_____

_____

Do You Know...

why names were important in the Old Testament?
In biblical times, to know someone's name was to have power over that person or object. For instance, in the Book of Genesis, the first human is given the power of naming the plants, animals, birds, and fishes. This established that humans had power over these beings. To have a name changed also was very significant. Changing a person's name changed his or her identity—who he or she was. So, for Abram's name to be changed to Abraham is very important. It shows the new role of Abraham—he is called to lead a nation. It also shows that God has power over Abraham because it is God who changed his name.

> *The Jews took up stones again to stone him. Jesus*
> *replied, "I have shown you many good works from the*
> *Father. For which of these are you going to stone me?"*
> *The Jews answered, "It is not for a good work that we*
> *are going to stone you, but for blasphemy, because you,*
> *though only a human being, are making yourself God."*
> *Jesus answered, "Is it not written in your law, 'I said, you*
> *are gods'? If those to whom the word of God came were*
> *called 'gods'—and the scripture cannot be annulled—can*
> *you say that the one whom the Father has sanctified and*
> *sent into the world is blaspheming because I said, 'I am*
> *God's Son'? If I am not doing the works of my Father,*
> *then do not believe me. But if I do them, even though*
> *you do not believe me, believe the works, so that you*
> *may know and understand that the Father is in me and*
> *I am in the Father." Then they tried to arrest him again,*
> *but he escaped from their hands.*

John 10:31-39

Jesus argues with the Jews effectively by using the very laws the Jews accuse him of breaking. Jesus also makes the point that a person's actions tell us who that person is.

What recent action would tell someone that you are a daughter or son of God?

_____

_____

_____

_____

_____

_____

Fifth Saturday of Lent— March 31

Powerful leaders like Jesus not only inspire admiration, but sometimes they also inspire fear. Jewish religious leaders feared Jesus.

> *So the chief priests and the Pharisees called a meeting of the council, and said, "What are we to do? This man is performing many signs. If we let him go on like this, everyone will believe in him, and the Romans will come and destroy both our holy place and our nation." But one of them, Caiaphas, who was high priest that year, said to them, "You know nothing at all! You do not understand that it is better for you to have one man die for the people than to have the whole nation destroyed." …So from that day on they planned to put him to death.*
> John 11:47-50, 53

How would you have told the chief priests and Pharisees to deal with Jesus?

_____

_____

_____

_____

_____

Do You Know...

who Caiaphas was?
Caiaphas was the chief priest in Jerusalem at the time of Jesus' trial, persecution, and death. The chief priest was in charge of all religious leaders. But as a religious leader, why would Caiaphas want Jesus killed? Jewish leaders felt threatened by Jesus and his teachings on love and care for the poor. They felt that if they could eliminate Jesus, their authority would no longer be questioned.

Make the Most of Holy Week!

Palm Sunday

On this day, originally called Passion Sunday, we recall Jesus' suffering and death in the Gospel account of the Passion.

◆ To prepare for the Palm Sunday liturgy, read Luke 22:14—23:56.

Holy Thursday

As he shared the Passover meal with his apostles, Jesus celebrated the Last Supper, telling the apostles that the bread they were eating was his Body, and the wine that they were drinking was his Blood. This was the first celebration of the Eucharist.

◆ Read the account in Mark 14:12-25.

When they were together for the Passover meal, Jesus washed the feet of his apostles to show them that they were to serve others.

◆ Read the account in John 13:1-20.

On Thursday of Holy Week, Christians share this special meal and repeat this special gesture during the Mass of the Lord's Supper.

◆ Be bread for others. Donate food or your time to a local food pantry.
◆ Commit a random act of kindness. Extend kindness to someone you don't know or someone you don't like.
◆ Volunteer to be one of the parishioners whose feet will be washed at the Mass of the Lord's Supper.

Good Friday

On this day of mourning, we remember the suffering and death of Jesus. The Church reenacts the passion and death of Jesus.

◆ Make a special effort this year to participate in your parish's Good Friday services.

◆ Find ways to fast today. You can fast not only from food, but from playing video games, shopping, watching TV. Think of the best ways for you to fast.

◆ Christians believe that Jesus hung on the cross for three hours—from noon to 3:00 p.m. Spend some time during these hours thinking about the sacrifice Jesus made for us and some sacrifices you might make for others.

◆ Because this is a day of mourning, visit the grave of a deceased relative or friend.

Holy Saturday, the Easter Vigil

This Mass, celebrated on the evening of Holy Saturday, begins in darkness to remind us of the darkness of death and also of the darkness at the beginning of time. We light the Easter Candle to symbolize that it is Jesus who breaks through this darkness as the Light of the World.

◆ Be light to the world! Light up someone's day. Visit a person in a nursing home. Buy an Easter plant for someone. Prepare a food basket for someone less fortunate than you. Wash windows. Clean your room.

Easter Sunday

This is the most important day of the Church year. If it weren't for the resurrection of Jesus, the other events that we celebrate as Church would be meaningless. It is on this day that we again say, "Alleluia, Christ is risen!"

◆ Read Matthew 28:1-15 to learn about Jesus' resurrection.

What one word or phrase captures your understanding of each of the events that occurred from Palm Sunday to Easter Sunday?

Palm Sunday _____

Holy Thursday _____

Good Friday _____

Holy Saturday, the Easter Vigil _____

Easter Sunday _____

Check out what Judas Iscariot says.

> *Six days before the Passover Jesus came to Bethany,*
> *the home of Lazarus, whom he had raised from the dead.*
> *There they gave a dinner for him. Martha served, and*
> *Lazarus was one of those at the table with him. Mary*
> *took a pound of costly perfume made of pure nard,*
> *anointed Jesus' feet, and wiped them with her hair. The*
> *house was filled with the fragrance of perfume. But Judas*
> *Iscariot, one of his disciples (the one who was about to*
> *betray him), said, "Why was this perfume not sold for*
> *three hundred denarii and the money given to the poor?"*
> *…Jesus said, "Leave her alone. She bought it so that*
> *she might keep it for the day of my burial. You always*
> *have the poor with you, but you do not always have me."*
> John 12:1-5, 7-8

Judas, who was believed to have been the disciples' treasurer, challenged Mary's use of her money, but then he sold Jesus for silver. Interesting!

How do you feel about money? How do you use it?

_____

_____

_____

Do You Know...

why Passover is so important to the Jews?
Passover is one of the most important Jewish religious feasts. The first Passover occurred during the time of Moses, when God sent plagues to convince Pharaoh to let the Israelites leave Egypt and the slavery that they endured there. The final plague by God was to kill all Egyptian firstborn sons. To save their own sons, the Israelites were told to kill a lamb and smear the blood of the lamb over the doorposts of their homes. When the angel of the Lord saw the blood, it would pass over that house. Every year Jews remember this important promise by God and celebrate Passover.

Have you ever entered a room where you got a strange sense that something was going on, but you didn't know what? Here the disciples are puzzled because Jesus seems troubled and they don't know why.

> ...Jesus was troubled in spirit, and declared,
> "Very truly, I tell you, one of you will betray me." The
> disciples looked at one another, uncertain of whom he
> was speaking. One of his disciples—the one whom
> Jesus loved—was reclining next to him; Simon Peter
> therefore motioned to him to ask Jesus of whom
> he was speaking. So while reclining next to Jesus, he
> asked him, "Lord, who is it?" Jesus answered, "It is the
> one to whom I give this piece of bread when I have
> dipped it in the dish." So when he had dipped the piece
> of bread, he gave it to Judas son of Simon Iscariot. After
> he received the piece of bread, Satan entered into him.
> Jesus said to him, "Do quickly what you are going to do."
>
> John 13:21-27

Judas is about to betray Jesus. Describe a time when you felt betrayed.

_____

_____

_____

_____

_____

_____

_____

Come on. Bring it on. There is nothing that you can do to me because God is on my side! This is Isaiah's message.

"I gave my back to those who struck me,
*   and my cheeks to those who pulled out the beard;*
I did not hide my face
*   from insult and spitting.*
The Lord GOD helps me;
*   therefore I have not been disgraced;*
therefore I have set my face like flint,
*   and I know that I shall not be put to shame;*
*   he who vindicates me is near.*
Who will contend with me?
*   Let us stand up together.*
Who are my adversaries?
*   Let them confront me.*
It is the Lord GOD who helps me...."

Isaiah 50:6-9

How do you feel when you are teased, insulted, or hurt? How difficult is it to remember that God helps you?

_____

_____

_____

_____

Do You Know...

what the Triduum is?
The period beginning with the Mass of the Lord's Supper on Holy Thursday evening and ending on Easter Sunday evening is called the Triduum. The word comes from Latin words meaning three days. These three days celebrate Christ's institution of the Eucharist, his passion and death, and his resurrection from the dead. There are no more meaningful celebrations than those the Church celebrates during the Triduum. See for yourself! Plan to participate.

Holy Thursday—April 5

As Christians we believe in God's providence—God's divine guidance in our life. Prayer and reflection help us to figure out what God is calling us to do. Jesus had a purpose, a mission for his life.

> ...[Jesus] stood up to read, and the scroll of the prophet Isaiah was given to him. He unrolled the scroll and found the place where it was written:
>> "The Spirit of the Lord is upon me,
>> because he has anointed me
>>> to bring good news to the poor.
>> He has sent me to proclaim release to the captives,
>>> and recovery of sight to the blind,
>>> to let the oppressed go free,
>> to proclaim the year of the Lord's favor."
>
> And he rolled up the scroll, gave it back to the attendant, and sat down. The eyes of all in the synagogue were fixed on him. Then he began to say to them, "Today this scripture has been fulfilled in your hearing."
>
> Luke 4:16-21

What do you think God is calling you to be or do?

_____

_____

_____

_____

Do You Know...

what's on the menu for a Passover feast?
Roast lamb—to remind the Jewish people of the lambs slaughtered so their blood could be sprinkled on the doorposts of their homes
Unleavened bread—as a reminder that as the Jews rushed to escape Egypt, they didn't have time to let their bread rise
Bitter herbs—to remind Jews that their experience was at times bitter
Wine—to celebrate the good times in the Jews' relationship with God

2 Good Friday—April 6

Did you ever hear the phrase, "to add insult to injury"? The inscription that Pilate put on the cross was intended to make fun of Jesus—to add insult to injury.

> ...So they took Jesus; and carrying the cross by himself, he went out to what is called The Place of the Skull, which in Hebrew is called Golgotha. There they crucified him, and with him two others, one on either side, with Jesus between them. Pilate also had an inscription written and put on the cross. It read, "Jesus of Nazareth, the King of the Jews."
>
> John 19:16-19

Look at a crucifix. See Pilate's inscription abbreviated in the initials *INRI*. (*I* for *Jesus*, *N* for *Nazareth*, *R* for *Rex* or *King*, *I* for *Jews*).

Who's Who?

Dietrich Bonhoeffer (1906-1945), a German theologian, suffered a fate similar to that of Jesus. Bonhoeffer had been arrested for helping Jews to escape the Nazis. He was sent to prison and eventually to a concentration camp. There, on April 9, he received a message that stated, "Prisoner Bonhoeffer, get ready and come with us." He said to a fellow prisoner, "This is the end, for me the beginning of life...." He was hanged with several others, including members of his family, who had taken part in the rescue of Jews.

What title or initials would you have inscribed on the cross?

_____

_____

_____

_____

_____

_____

_____

_____

_____

But on the first day of the week, at early dawn, they came to the tomb, taking the spices that they had prepared. They found the stone rolled away from the tomb, but when they went in, they did not find the body. While they were perplexed about this, suddenly two men in dazzling clothes stood beside them. The women were terrified and bowed their faces to the ground, but the men said to them, "Why do you look for the living among the dead? He is not here, but has risen. Remember how he told you, while he was still in Galilee, that the Son of Man must be handed over to sinners, and be crucified, and on the third day rise again." Then they remembered his words, and returning from the tomb, they told all this to the eleven and to all the rest.

Luke 24:1-9

SURPRISE!

HAPPY BIRTH

Knowing that it cannot even come close to the surprise and amazement of the women who were looking for Jesus, describe the best surprise of your life. Who were among the first people you told? Why?

_____

_____

_____

_____

_____

_____

_____

57

Point of Interest

Meet the *Oschter Haws*!

Even when we no longer believe in the Easter bunny, the Easter season still includes Easter eggs, chocolate bunnies, and baskets. Where did all these traditions begin?

The egg has traditionally been a symbol of new life. Human beings are created from a fertilized egg. Many animals are either hatched or evolve from an egg. What better symbol than an egg to show the new life that Jesus gives to us through his death and resurrection?

Did you know that originally eggs were painted with bright colors to represent the sunlight of spring? These colored eggs were used in Easter-egg-rolling contests and given as gifts. The custom of giving eggs as well as Easter gifts developed in Germany. To hold the eggs and even hide them in a kind of hide-and-go-seek game, baskets were used.

Different ways of decorating eggs developed throughout the world. *Pysanki*, one of the most famous egg-decorating techniques, comes from the Ukrainians and has been adopted by many other cultures. Melted beeswax is used to cover parts of the egg. The egg is then dipped in different dye baths. After each color is added, wax is painted over the area where the color is to remain. Eventually a pattern of lines and colors emerge into a work of art!

Where do we get the tradition of the chocolate Easter bunny? The rabbit, like the egg, symbolizes life. It is an incredibly fertile animal. That's why there are so many rabbits running around people's backyards! This fertility means new life, just like the new life we receive upon our death because Jesus died and rose from the dead.

In the 1500s, the Germans began to use the rabbit as an Easter symbol. Then, in the early 1800s, they celebrated this symbol by making Easter bunnies that could be eaten. These first edible Easter bunnies were made out of pastry and sugar.

In America, the Easter bunny took on an even greater importance for children. In Pennsylvania Dutch areas during the 1700s, a visit by the *Oschter Haws,* or Easter Bunny, was considered almost as important as a visit from Santa Claus. The children believed that if they were good, the Oschter Haws would lay a nest of colored eggs. To prepare, boys would use their caps and girls their bonnets to make nests for the rabbit. This custom eventually evolved into the modern-day Easter basket.

How do these symbols connect with our beliefs as Christians? Each Easter symbol traces its roots to the belief in new life. As Christians, that is our ultimate belief. Death is overcome by life. Jesus' death on a cross on Good Friday leads to his resurrection from the grave on Easter Sunday. The symbols of Easter help us to celebrate this new life.

Now, go find that Easter Basket!

Egg Artistry

If you'd like to learn more about the Ukrainian egg-decorating technique, do a web search with the word *Pysanki*. Then create a design, either modeled after a *Pysanki* design or of your own invention, in this outline of an egg.

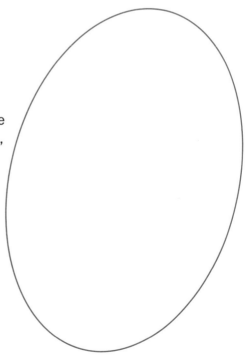

Easter Sunday—April 8

The countdown to Easter is over. You have arrived with Peter at an empty tomb. Jesus has risen! Alleluia!

Then Simon Peter came, following him, and went into the tomb. He saw the linen wrappings lying there, and the cloth that had been on Jesus' head, not lying with the linen wrappings but rolled up in a place by itself. Then the other disciple, who reached the tomb first, also went in, and he saw and believed; for as yet they did not understand the scripture, that he must rise from the dead.

John 20:6-9

All of creation shouts for joy! Take a walk today or look outside your window. Record here all the signs of new life. What does it mean to you that Jesus has promised us new life after death?

_____

_____

_____

_____

Do You Know...

that Easter is a movable feast?
We celebrate Easter on the first Sunday after the first full moon following the vernal equinox, the first day of spring. Easter can be celebrated on any of thirty-five dates, from March 22 to April 25.

Continuing the Journey

Lent has been a time to pray, do good works, reflect, and build your trust in a God who will one day lead you to resurrection. When you face difficult times or difficult situations, it will help you to remember that Jesus did, too. He was sustained in those times through prayer and trust in God's plan for him.

Here's a simple prayer to remind you of your Lenten journey to Easter 2007. Repeat it often as you continue to walk with Jesus.

Risen Jesus, help me always to remember that when I walk with you, my journey will bring me to new light and life.

Answers for **Decode the Stations of the Cross!** (Page 19)

2nd Station:

↑≋Ⅿ ∿▢✪♙♙ 🖐♙ ●✠🖐♌ ◆➜✪■ ☺Ⅿ♙◆♙

The cross is laid upon Jesus.

4th Station:

☺Ⅿ♙◆♙ ○Ⅿ♍↑♙ ≋🖐♙ ○✪↑≋Ⅿ▢ ○✠▢◆

Jesus meets his mother, Mary.

7th Station:

☺Ⅿ♙◆♙ ⚹✠●●♙ ⚹✪▢ ↑≋Ⅿ ♙Ⅿ∿✪■♌ ↑🖐○Ⅿ

Jesus falls for the second time.

11th Station:

☺Ⅿ♙◆♙ 🖐♙ ■✠🖐●Ⅿ♌ ↑✪ ↑≋Ⅿ ∿▢✪♙♙

Jesus is nailed to the cross.

14th Station:

☺Ⅿ♙◆♙ 🖐♙ ●✠🖐♌ 🖐■ ↑≋Ⅿ ↑✪○♌

Jesus is laid in the tomb.

15th Station:

☺Ⅿ♙◆♙ ▢🖐♙Ⅿ♙ ⚹▢✪○ ↑≋Ⅿ ♌Ⅿ✠♌

Jesus rises from the dead.

Answers for **Play the Catholic Millionaire Game!** (Pages 34 and 35)

1. c—Even though it would seem logical that a baker invented the pretzel, it was, in fact, a monk who began this tradition in the year 610.

2. a—The monk who invented the pretzel out of leftover dough in the monastery kitchen intended to make something that would remind people of prayer. He folded strips of dough to look like arms folded in prayer.

3. d—The tradition of bending dough into the shape of praying arms began in Germany.

4. d—Believe it or not, people in the United States consume 400 million pounds of pretzels each year. That's a lot of pretzels and probably involves a lot of soda to wash them down!

5. c—Nutmeg is not traditionally an ingredient found in pretzels. Water, flour, and salt are the key ingredients.

6. a—The bright colors traditionally used to dye Easter eggs represent the bright sunshine of spring.

7. b—Each European country has a unique and traditional way to decorate or color Easter eggs. In Greece, the traditional color is red to represent the blood of Jesus as he suffered and died on the cross.

8. c—The Ukrainian way to decorate Easter eggs is called *Pysanki*. In the past, plant material was used to cover parts of the eggs as they were placed in different colors of dye. Today, melted wax and modern tools are used to achieve the characteristic and incredible designs.

9. b—Because the rabbit is so fertile (as most farmers and gardeners know!), it is a sign and symbol of life.

10. c—The egg also symbolizes new life.

Where to Find What

Do You Know...

Who's Who?